While It Is Day
Early Will i Seek God

by

Foster Ofori

Contents

Introduction

Have you paid attention to what is happening in our world today? Unemployment, political instability, corruption, wars, rumors of war, earthquakes, hurricanes, diseases, terrorism, gun shooting and violence, and sudden deaths. While these things have always occurred throughout human history and often go through cycles in individual regions of the world, it seems evident that these events are becoming more prolific.

Some have claimed that these things are nothing new, but rather they appear to be so because we now live in an age of mass media, whereas before, if thousands died in some natural disaster or war, the rest of the world may not have heard about it. However, Niall Ferguson's book, titled *The War of the World: Twentieth-Century Conflict and the Descent of the West*, shows indisputably that the 20th century was the bloodiest, most destructive century in human history.

We are currently only a fifth of the way into the 21st century; however, based on world events such as COVID-19 and the several events projecting global warming, along with seeming economic wars, this century seems on track to surpass the previous one.

Regardless of how one may feel about all this, a reading of the Bible and end time events indicates death and destruction on a scale paralleled to all previous centuries combined is looming on the not-so-distant horizon.

In America, during the past year, we have seen a rapid decline in the loss of their freedoms, chaos in many of their major cities, and the nation seemingly on the edge of a second Civil War. However, the name is also a misnomer, for there is nothing civil about war.

Within just a year, in America and Canada, nations founded a decline in religious freedom. Under the guise of a pandemic, we have seen the closing down and shuttering of the vast majority of the churches. Amazingly, unlike in countries such as China which uses the threat of force to keep the church hidden underground, the local and denominational leaders in America willingly acquiesced and closed their church doors. While some could argue that such a thing may have been necessary for a short period of time at the very beginning of the pandemic, what was promised to be a short-term event of several weeks has now gone on for over a year.

In states like California, churches are threatened with fines of tens of thousands of dollars for conducting services beyond a mere handful of people, despite having auditoriums capable of seating thousands. Moreover, they are also being told by the state how they are permitted to conduct their services, with no public prayer, singing, or even specials.

Prior to 2020, if such suggestions and orders had happened to America's churches, it would've brought forth mocking laughter, saying such a thing could never happen here. But it has.

Additionally, it seems that America is becoming more and more under police control. In California, a police helicopter and boats swarmed a soul surfer who was out in the ocean for violating the state's lockdown orders. In Colorado, a man was handcuffed and arrested in front of his children for the unspeakable sin of allowing them to play outside at a park when no one else was around. In New York City, Jewish playgrounds were locked and chained, and the mayor forbade them from allowing funerals, threatening to arrest the rabbis and place them in jail.

Now, we see political leaders of one political party attempting to demonize all those who disagree with them by threatening them with the titles domestic terrorist, members of a hate group, and white supremacist. Ironically, they even claim that members of minority groups are also white supremacists for adhering to basic Christian beliefs such as the sanctity of life, personal liberty, and traditional marriage. If things continue on their current track, it seems political leaders may actually call for jailing not just their political opponents but also those who disagree with their political beliefs and put them in a gulag like what happened in the former Soviet Union or Kim Jong-Un's political prison camps.

It certainly seems as if, like what happened in the book of Job, God has given Satan permission to go forth and destroy not just an individual but America as a whole. At this point, no one knows how long this time of testing will last and how long we will be examined.

All this chaos and confusion have resulted in vast numbers of people being filled with terror, confusion, and anxiety. Some health authorities have stated that mental health issues, increased domestic violence, alcohol, and drug abuse have all skyrocketed due to anxiety issues caused by the government lockdowns. Nevertheless, these issues are actually having a higher death toll than the virus itself.

Economically, many people find themselves on the verge of being evicted from their homes and losing jobs because of government edicts as they wonder when it will all end.

All these things have resulted in a world that desperately seeks answers or solutions to the problems.

Many researchers and healthcare professionals have done their best to help in this area, and yet we still experience problems. Some have consulted other powers - Illuminati, new age priests, witches, and false prophets in a desperate attempt to get answers.

While there is a natural tendency, when faced with any kind of seeming emergency such as we see today, to irrationally latch onto anything that seems to offer even a glimmer of hope, unfortunately, the vast majority of things people are turning to have a failed track record regarding the record of success the people are longing for.

The reason is, all these things are either man-made worldly solutions or baubles offered by the Prince of the powers of the air, the one who led the initial rebellion in Heaven, Satan himself. All these things are contrary to God and His plan and commandments, and as such, they can only bring about failure and destruction, just as they always have whenever and wherever they are tried.

With all the problems in the world, there is only one solution to all the questions plaguing us. It can only be found in a single book, the Bible, the written word of God which points us to its "counterpart," the incarnate Word of God, Jesus Christ, the Saviour of the world.

Ultimately, all these problems will only cease at the coming of the Prince of Peace when he sits on his earthly throne in Jerusalem. However, until then, scriptures present us with ways for us to live as "the sons of God, without rebuke, in the midst of a crooked and perverse nation, among whom ye shine as lights in the world" (Philippians 2:15).

The Bible tells us in Romans 8:28 that "And we know that in all things God works for the good of those who love him, who have been called according to his purpose." This is one of the most amazing verses in the Bible. However, like all verses, it is important for us to "Study to shew thyself approved unto God, a workman that needeth not to be ashamed, rightly dividing the word of truth," to ensure exactly what this verse is saying, and who it is speaking to.

A fatal mistake many people make when reading the Scriptures is assuming that every verse applies to all people at all times. This mistake is the primary source of the vast majority of confusion and controversies over doctrines that seemingly contradict themselves. It is a truism and has often been said that the Bible never contradicts itself; however, we would be deceiving ourselves if we don't say there are verses that appear to do so. Notice I said appear. In other words, there is no real contradiction, but only the appearance of such.

There are many reasons for this, but again, the primary reason is a lack of understanding of who is being addressed in the book or passage. It is important to understand that while all of the Bible was written FOR us, all of the Bible was not written TO us. For example, God gave Noah a very direct command to build a boat to save his life and that of his family and another very clear command to Abraham to sacrifice his firstborn son and offer him up for a burnt offering.

It would be the height of folly, and in the case of the command given to Abraham, a tragedy was someone to read these passages and assume this is a commandment required for salvation or something God wants us to do today. It has been said that if you take a verse out of context or read it haphazardly, you can make it say anything you want to.

To illustrate this, a preacher told of an individual who supposedly wanted God to speak to him from the Scriptures, but he didn't want the man to have any part in teaching him what God wanted him to do. Therefore, he reasoned that he would randomly flip back and forth through pages of Scripture then place his finger on a verse and that if God was really speaking to them, that passage would tell him what God wanted him to do.

On his first attempt, his finger landed on Matthew 27:5. "And he cast down the pieces of silver in the temple, and departed, and went and hanged himself."

Shocked at what this verse stated and became terrified at its implications, he reasoned that perhaps he did this wrong and would try it again. So once again, he randomly placed his finger on a verse, and this time it was Luke 10:37, which said, "Then said Jesus unto him, Go, and do thou likewise."

By now, he was terrified because, based on his own criteria for how he expected God to speak to him, Jesus had just told him to go and kill himself. Surely that couldn't be true, he reasoned. After all, isn't suicide a sin? He thought he would take one more stab at it, and this time imagine the anxiety he felt when he came upon this verse.

> "... Then said Jesus unto him, That thou doest,
> do quickly." (John 13:27)

Of course, such a thing probably never happened, but it illustrates the point about understanding who a passage is addressed to.

In the case of Romans 8:28, the Apostle Paul makes it plain who this verse is addressed to in Romans 1:7. "To all that be in Rome, beloved of God, called to be saints: Grace to you and peace from God our Father, and the Lord Jesus Christ."

In other words, Romans 8:28 is a verse for those who are born again, having put their faith and trust in the finished work of Jesus Christ. While God certainly wants all people to come to him and is not willing that any should perish, this does not mean that everything good that happens in the life of a lost person is for their own good. God may choose to use it as a teaching tool in an attempt to prod them to lay aside their pride and accept what he says is necessary for salvation, but God is under no obligation to do so. However, when it comes to his children, that is a different matter entirely.

God takes care of His own. He always makes sure that those who believe and love Him are protected and saved from the enemy's trap. This does not mean they will live a life free of strife, far from it. In fact, Jesus warned his disciples that if the world persecuted Him, they would do the same to them. He also said matter of factly, "In the world ye shall have tribulation." The scripture also stated in Job that "man is born unto trouble as the sparks fly upward." History validates these scriptures, as does a reading of Fox's Book of Martyrs, along with the Voice of the Martyrs monthly newsletter.

God has never promised a life down here on earth of flowery beds of ease; what makes Romans 8:28 so great is that unlike people in the world who do not know God and are lost, a Christian has the certainty that comes from God's promise that everything we do will work together for good.

However, to obtain the full benefits of that promise, we need to live our lives as born-again believers having a strong personal relationship with him. This is why it says, "those who love him, who have been called according to his purpose."

It does no good for God to send us a blessing if we don't know what it is or how to appropriate it fully. It has been reported in the news in the United States that when the government sent out $1,200 stimulus checks in the summer of 2020, it was sent out to some people as a pre-paid debit card because they didn't have a bank account. When the letter came, some people assumed it was just junk mail, so they threw the envelopes away. They received a blessing of thousands of dollars, but it did them no good because they did not read the newspaper articles about how the funds were coming and didn't know what to do with this gift.

There will be many problems happening on earth, but God will continue to fulfill His promise by watching over his people and ensuring that it is all going to work out for their good. However, just like those who threw all that money in the trash, as Christians, we must be sure to "follow the news" so we understand how to avail ourselves of this protection and blessings.

God's newspaper is the Bible, and to ensure we are up to date on God's instructions, we need to read the Bible and seek God and have a personal walk with Him.

In Revelation 3:20, God describes a church in John's day that was in the city of Laodicea. Jesus states something shocking. "Behold, I stand at the door, and knock: if any man hear my voice, and open the door, I will come in to him, and will sup with him, and he with me."

Contrary to what many think, this verse is not directed at a lost person, although there is nothing wrong with using this passage in an applicational sense. No, this plea by Jesus is directed to a local church made up of individual blood-washed believers. He states that although he is outside of this church, he is knocking and asking for permission to come in. How tragic this is.

It means that although this church may have had all the trappings that indicated it was a Christian church, inwardly, Jesus, the head of the church, had been kicked out. However, he says he is gladly ready to come back if they will only open the door. Someone once said, "If you don't feel as close to God as you used to, who moved?"

No man can solve the problems on the earth except the Lord Jesus Christ, who has all the power and authority. However, to obtain this power and authority and learn how to utilize it, we must allow him into our lives so that we can have a heart-to-heart conversation with him. Anyone can study and learn something about somebody they admire as people do with celebrities or political leaders they respect. However, if you want to know somebody instead of knowing about them, you must have the kind of relationship where you spend personal one-on-one time together in both quantity and quality time.

God is not the one who moved. Therefore, if we want to remain close, we are the ones who must move closer to get to know him. We do this by reading his word and allowing Him to speak to us, but we also must actively seek Him early while we have the strength and life to do so. Go to a nursing home, and you will find many people filled with regrets over not spending their earlier years seeking after God and knowing Him instead of just knowing about Him.

So come along and let us journey together as we learn about what exactly it means to seek God and how we do this. If you have never done so in a real way, you are in for an exciting time of your life that will make your relationship with God more alive and vibrant than it has ever been.

Chapter 1
Seeking God

Seek ye the LORD while he may be found, call ye upon him while he is near: (Isaiah 55:6)

In the beginning, Adam and Eve frequently sought-after God and had a marvelous relationship with him. Genesis 2:19 indicates that this relationship was so close that God, the one who created the entire universe and all the responsibilities this entailed, took time to sit down with Adam and watched while all the animals were paraded before him, and Adam was tasked with giving them their names.

"And out of the ground the LORD God formed every beast of the field, and every fowl of the air; and brought them unto Adam to see what he would call them: and whatsoever Adam called every living creature, that was the name thereof." (Genesis 2:19)

Notice the phrasing that states that God wanted to "see what he would call them," indicating that this was something that was pretty important to God. In our personal relationships, if we truly love and care about somebody, we take an interest in what is important to them, even if it is not something, we are particularly fond of. For example, a man who loves sports and fast cars, if he knows his wife loves needlepoint, will take time out of his schedule to go to the hobby store with her or even craft shows featuring needlepoint. The same is true for the wife regarding her husband's interests.

However, this relationship changed following Adam and Eve partaking of the fruit from the tree of good and evil knowledge. Whereas before they delighted in spending time seeking after God, Scripture states in Genesis 3:8-9, "And they heard the voice of the LORD God walking in the garden in the cool of the day: and Adam and his wife hid themselves from the presence of the LORD God amongst the trees of the garden. And the LORD God called unto Adam, and said unto him, Where art thou?"

Something had definitely changed between the two events. Paul describes this change in attitude in Romans 3:11 while explaining why we do not seek after God in our natural state, which is why man is incapable of saving himself. "There is none that understandeth, there is none that seeketh after God."

David said in Psalm 10:4, "The wicked, through the pride of his countenance, will not seek after God: God is not in all his thoughts."

While a lost person will have a certain longing over the knowledge there is something lacking in their life, the relationship Adam once held; they do not have the same desire as a Christian who is a "new creature" in Christ. If you are born again, then one of the fruits of your salvation is having a desire to seek after God, not in some vague sense, but by wanting to pursue a relationship with him like Adam had.

I am convinced that most Christians fail in areas of Christian life because pastors and other Christian leaders instruct them on what to do in their life but fail to tell them exactly how to do it.

For example, how many times have you heard sermons telling us to read our Bible and pray? We respond with a hearty amen, indicating we agree with that sentiment. However, why is there then a disconnect between the universal agreement in this area and Christians actually doing it? I believe it is an act of laziness to simply chalk it up to an act of rebellion on the part of the individuals. I believe there are many who long to seek after God and have a relationship with him, but they simply don't know how because no one has ever taken the time to teach them.

We have read the Scriptures that tell us about the importance of and commands us to seek after God, but what exactly does this mean? Websters 1828 American Dictionary of the English Language provides us with a definition to help us understand what the word was originally intended to mean. Unlike modern dictionaries, which frequently change the meaning in order to become more politically correct, Websters 1828 frequently cites Scripture to validate the definition. Here is how it defines the word seek:

1. To go in search or quest of; to look for; to search for by going from place to place. The man asked him, saying, what seekest thou? And he said, I seek my brethren. Genesis 37:15-16.

2. To inquire for; to ask for; to solicit; to endeavor to find or gain by any means. The young lions roar after their prey and seek their meat from God. Psalms 104:21. He found no place for repentance, though he sought it carefully with tears. Hebrews 12:1 Others tempting him sought of him a sign. Luke 11:16.

3. Seek is followed sometimes by out or after. To seek out properly implies to look for a specific thing among a number. But in general, the use of out and after with seek is unnecessary and inelegant.

To seek God, his name, or his face, in Scripture, to ask for his favor, direction and assistance. Psalm 83:16.

God seeks men when he fixes his love on them, and by his word and Spirit, and the righteousness of Christ, reclaims and recovers them from their miserable condition as sinners. Ezekiel 34:6. Psa 119:2. Luke 15:8.

To seek after the life or soul, to attempt by arts or machinations, or to attempt to destroy or ruin. Psalm 35:4.

To seek peace or judgment, to endeavor to promote it, or to practice it. Psalm 34:14. Isaiah 1:17.

To seek an altar, temple, or habitation, to frequent it; to restore to it often. 2 Chronicles 1:1. Amos 5:4.

To seek out God's works, to endeavor to understand them. Psalm 111:2.

As we can see, seeking involves far more than merely looking for something. It involves doing so with a passion that causes the individual to be consumed with doing whatever it takes or whatever the cost to obtain that which they are seeking after. They will have an insatiable hunger that cannot be quenched until their soul is satisfied. Does that describe your desire to seek after God?

Seeking God means doing whatever it takes to be in His presence or face. In the Old Testament, you will see it was common for kings wanting to fight each other to say something like, "come, let us see one another in the face." In other words, they were going to get up close and personal.

In a similar manner, seeking after God does not mean doing something half-heartedly, like doing an online search to see which stores carry a particular item you are looking to purchase at some future date. Instead, it means having a hungry desire to look each other directly in the eye, inches from each other. In loving relationships, this is seen by couples looking at each other with googly eyes with their noses almost touching each other.

This understanding of the intensity intimated behind the word "seek" helps us understand why it seems like Christians seeking after God do not see any real change in their life or nation. For instance, consider a verse that many Christians frequently cite expressing a desire for America to return to her Christian roots.

"If my people, who are called by my name, will humble themselves and pray and seek my face and turn from their wicked ways, then I will hear from heaven, and I will forgive their sin and will heal their land." (2 Chronicles 7:14)

This verse has been proclaimed in numerous churches, especially around Independence Day, yet it seems nothing ever changes. Why? God's people respond to the sermons by confessing their sins and that of America, but why are we still in the spiritual state we find ourselves in today? It is because we are not seeking the fervency demanded by the meaning of the word. We need to have the attitude of Rachel when she responded to Jacob regarding her being childless when she said, "Give me children, or else I die" (Genesis 30:1).

God is always with us. He is omnipresent and always waiting for his children to run to him with open arms. We are the ones who have put the distance between us, and we are the only ones who can close the gap. Therefore, it is up to us to continuously seek Him with a passion that says, "I need to seek you, and I'm going to do whatever it takes to seek you and remain in your presence, even if it kills me."

When we seek him with this intensity and fervency, we will not have to obey him by going down a checklist and doing things in a methodical, almost robotic way. Reading your Bible and spending time in prayer will not seem like an obligation but rather something you must do to satisfy the hunger in your heart.

In seeking the face of God with this level of passion, we will be consumed with having a natural desire to walk according to His will, then all the other things in the Christian life will fall neatly into place. We will obey His word, be sanctified, live a holy life, hate sin, and cheerfully receive directions from Him.

This will enable us to tap into his strength, enabling us to become more singularly focused on our purpose. Jesus said, "without me ye can do nothing." There is no "without me you can do nothing, except," in that verse. It means precisely what it says.

God, our Father, wants us to come closer to Him and recognize Him as the Almighty and Supreme creator and ruler of the universe. While it is impossible for us to truly comprehend the awesomeness of God and the sheer, radiant power of his holiness while in this mortal body of flesh, seeking him will enable us to come closer.

Three examples in the Scripture illustrate this point.

"In the year that king Uzziah died I saw also the Lord sitting upon a throne, high and lifted up, and his train filled the temple. Above it stood the seraphims: each one had six wings; with twain he covered his face, and with twain he covered his feet, and with twain he did fly. And one cried unto another, and said, Holy, holy, holy, is the LORD of hosts: the whole earth is full of his glory. And the posts of the door moved at the voice of him that cried, and the house was filled with smoke. **Then said I, Woe is me! for I am undone; because I am a man of unclean lips, and I dwell in the midst of a people of unclean lips: for mine eyes have seen the King, the LORD of hosts.**" (Isaiah 6:1-5)

Notice that when the prophet Isaiah was carried up into heaven's throne room and saw God face-to-face, he was suddenly confronted with how vile his sinful state was when laid alongside the raw holiness of Almighty God. This realization brought about a great humbleness that caused him to fall down on his face. Following this encounter, he was emboldened to go forth and proclaim God's judgment throughout the land with confidence, despite God telling him that no one would listen to what he had to say (Isaiah 6:11).

Now let's see a similar encounter with God by the Apostle John, of whom it was said multiple times that he was "the disciple whom Jesus loved."

"And I turned to see the voice that spake with me. And being turned, I saw seven golden candlesticks; And in the midst of the seven candlesticks one like unto the Son of man, clothed with a garment down to the foot, and girt about the paps with a golden girdle. His head and his hairs were white like wool, as white as snow; and his eyes were as a flame of fire; And his feet like unto fine brass, as if they burned in a furnace; and his voice as the sound of many waters. And he had in his right hand seven stars: and out of his mouth went a sharp twoedged sword: and his countenance was as the sun shineth in his strength. And when I saw him, I fell at his feet as dead. And he laid his right hand upon me, saying unto me, Fear not; I am the first and the last:" (Revelation 1:12-17)

During Jesus' time on earth, John was not just one of the twelve but one of the so-called big three, Peter, James, and John. As such, he knew Jesus on a much more personal level and more intimately than the majority of the people living in Israel during that time. Yet despite this wonderful relationship, like Isaiah, when he saw Jesus Christ in his full glory, not as the Lamb of God but as the lion from the tribe of Judah, John stated that he fell down as one dead.

For our last verse, let's take a look at how creation itself responds when confronted with God's holiness.

"And I saw a great white throne, and him that sat on it, from whose face the earth and the heaven fled away; and there was found no place for them." (Revelation 20:11)

Even creation itself had the same reaction John and Isaiah did. When you seek after God, you begin to truly experience this holiness and see the contrast between God and yourself.

Seeking God is an individual choice. Your parents, pastor, or friends cannot seek God for you; it is something you must do for yourself. While an individual can certainly be the recipient and be blessed by the prayers of others upon their life, would it not be far better to walk through life being blessed because of your walk with God instead of being dependent on others?

If you are to ever successfully seek after God the way God intends, you will need to come to the point where you realize there truly is a God in heaven and that he delights in answering your prayers. Not only that, when we pray and call out to him, it is not something that is a burden to him. We will never catch him on a bad day or at a time when he is too busy to give us his undivided attention. Quite the opposite, God sits up in heaven, longingly waiting for us to come to him with our needs and problems.

This is his specialty and something he delights in because it magnifies him and brings him glory when we do these things. The trials and overwhelming problems of this world often seek to crush and destroy us. For a lost person, these things truly can become overwhelming, which is why so many turn to things such as drugs, alcohol, or even suicide.

When a child of God seeks after their heavenly Father, it brings Him glory, for you are acknowledging your total submission to him as you acknowledge all good things come from him.

The presence of God gives us confidence and hope for the future. Flesh and blood cannot take us far, but the presence of God or seeking God in all things will lead us to a better destination. The presence of God comes when we seek Him.

We do this by praying and reading His word continuously and listening to men of God. When we do these things, God speaks to us. Jesus said anyone who seeks God shall find Him (Matthew 7:8). The prophet Jeremiah echoed this when he proclaimed, "And ye shall seek me, and find me, when ye shall search for me with all your heart (Jeremiah 29:13).

God is not far away from us. Look at Psalm 63:1

O God, thou art my God;
early will I seek thee:
my soul thirsteth for thee,
my flesh longeth for thee
in a dry and thirsty land,
where no water is

I have realized that God is always hiding, but he wants us to reach out to Him while he is also looking for me at the same time. Sometimes it may seem that there is a distance between God and us, but we can close this gap when we decide to get in touch with Him through prayers and reading the word. God's ears hear, and his mouth talks. Anytime we come closer, He will talk to us and tell us what to do.

When God called Moses at the burning bush, rather than jump up with excitement and having an arrogant attitude where he said to himself, "I always knew this time would come. I was born to be my people's deliverer and now it's time to show Pharaoh who's boss here;" Moses realized that he couldn't do anything by himself, so he told God he wasn't up to the task. God responded by reminding Moses that He was the one who made Moses' lips and he knew Moses' capabilities. Moses asked God to accompany him to the palace, and God told him he would let Aaron accompany him to speak on his behalf.

Seeking God also includes wholeheartedly setting the mind and heart upon Him. "Now set your heart and your soul to seek the LORD your God; arise therefore, and build ye the sanctuary of the LORD God, to bring the ark of the covenant of the LORD, and the holy vessels of God, into the house that is to be built to the name of the LORD" (1 Chronicles 22:19). We must seek God with all our souls and heart.

Chapter 2
When to seek God

In the previous chapter, we discussed the importance of seeking God if we ever hope to attain the fellowship and relationship mankind was created to enjoy with God in the garden of Eden. The question now becomes, when exactly is the best time to seek God. When I ask this question, I don't mean when in the sense of putting a date on your calendar. Obviously, when it comes to doing anything God wants us to do, the answer should always be immediate.

When I say when, I am referring to a specific part of your day. Before we get into it the actual time on your calendar, let me encourage you to first develop the mindset that seeking God is the most important thing you can do in your daily schedule. As such, like anything else we do that's important, it must be scheduled. If you have a job, you don't just go to work when you feel like it. While you may not have it written down, there is an expectation that you will leave your home at a certain time and then clock in and clock out at set hours established by your employer. When we have a doctor's appointment, we don't just decide that someday, at some time, we will just show up at the doctor's office, and hopefully, everything works out. No, we put the date and time on our calendar, and then everything else is scheduled around it because we know this is something that is important.

Years ago, a survey was done where preachers were asked to list what they thought were the ten most important responsibilities they had as a pastor. All of them placed spending time reading and studying the Bible and praying at the top of the list. They were then asked to take those same ten items and rank them one through ten by the amount of time they spent on each of these ten items. Amazingly, while prayer and Bible reading were at the top of the list of priorities, it came in dead last regarding the amount of time spent. Instead, other things such as counseling, administrative paperwork, hospital visits, etc., took up most of their schedule.

Part of the reason for this discrepancy involves our mindset. It comes down to what we truly believe is the most important, or if we just say a certain thing is important because we have been taught that is the answer we are expected to give.

Whenever this subject comes up, the answer I frequently hear is, "I want to seek God, read my Bible and pray, but I just don't have time. I am too busy." First, let me say that if that is really true, you are too busy, and something needs to be changed. However, upon closer examination, I have always found that their excuse is far from the truth.

To help someone with this, I recommend they sit down with a paper and pen and then account for every minute of their day from when they wake up to when they lay their head down on their pillow at night. It is easy to get them to take the challenge because they are positive; it will validate their excuse.

But when we go over the list, something quite interesting nearly always turns up. In the morning, there are gaps between when they wake up and start getting ready for work to when they walk out the door. It may be a few minutes here and there, but they do have some spare time. The same thing happens throughout the day with their breaks. Then when they get home, there is a time when they sit down and relax, followed by spending time reading the newspaper or watching the news on TV. Of course, there is also time taken up with social media or spending time with family or friends.

I am not saying it is wrong to do these things; instead, I am trying to point out that we really do have more time in our schedule for seeking God than we think we do. It is just a question of the importance we place on it compared to some of these other things. Someone once said in response to this excuse of "I just don't have time," that "You will always find time to do whatever is important to you."

Now that we have made the decision that seeking God is something we are going to schedule, where is the best time to put it?

Let me say that I agree with David when he says it is best to seek God early. "O God, thou art my God; early will I seek thee: my soul thirsteth for thee, my flesh longeth for thee in a dry and thirsty land, where no water is" (Psalm 63:1).

During the day, preferably before you do much of anything else, I believe it is the ideal time to seek after God in your personal walk with Him. There are several reasons for this. First, since seeking God is something to be done in private, rather than trying to force it into your schedule, especially if you have a family, when you get up before everyone else does, it is easier to have that quiet time with God before all the hustle and bustle comes once everyone else is getting ready for the day's events. I have found that no matter how sincere you are, once you wake up and everything starts happening, it is too easy to allow your seeking God to be crowded out by all the "necessary things" like brushing your teeth, shaving, taking a shower, getting dressed, eating breakfast, etc.

I also believe this helps develop a proper mindset that will carry you through the day. When you seek God early, you are telling yourself and God that he truly is first before anything else. I knew a preacher who decided that he would not have any physical food until after partaking in his spiritual food. He explained how this made sure he spent his time walking with God every day because on those days when his flesh didn't feel like seeking God, it wanted to satisfy its physical cravings for food, so he used this leverage to place his body under submission.

Additionally, when you put seeking after God in the middle of the day or at the close of the day, it can seem like more of an afterthought. "Oh yeah, God. I'll squeeze you in again," right before you lay your head on your pillow and fall asleep. Please understand, if you are truly unable to spend time with God in the morning, anytime is better than no time. I am just trying to suggest what time is generally the best for most people. That is also when Jesus spent time with the Father.

Once we have sought God and spent time with him by developing a relationship with him, that is not the end-all. As Christians, we do not love the world nor be partakers of its desires and pleasures, which is often contrary to God. "Love not the world, neither the things that are in the world. If any man love the world, the love of the Father is not in him" (1 John 2:15).

It does not mean that we are to spend so much time seeking God that we completely withdraw from the world. Jesus said in John 17:15, "I pray not that thou shouldest take them out of the world, but that thou shouldest keep them from the evil." We are to be in the world but not of the world.

We are called to be God's ambassadors in this foreign land known as the earth for a world that does not know God. Our citizenship is in Heaven, but we are to represent our King and country while down here by sharing the good news of salvation. We are to seek God as part of our preparation for service, but if we don't go forth, we are like a soldier who spends all his time in training and never fights the enemy. Such a one does his country no good when it is under attack.

When Jesus was asked why he was so devoted to his ministry on earth, he told them, "I must work the works of him that sent me, while it is day: the night cometh, when no man can work" (John 9:4). So what exactly is the "day" compared to the "night"? Jesus gave us the answer when he said in John 8:12, "Then spake Jesus again unto them, saying, I am the light of the world: he that followeth me shall not walk in darkness, but shall have the light of life." He then clarified that this age was referred to as living in prior to his second coming.

"As long as I am in the world, I am the light of the world." (John 9:5)

The period after the church is caught up in the rapture is referred to as a time of great spiritual darkness on the whole earth where Satan is given free rein over this planet. This was prophesied by Isaiah when he wrote, "For, behold, the darkness shall cover the earth, and gross darkness the people: but the LORD shall arise upon thee, and his glory shall be seen upon thee" (Isaiah 60:2).

Genesis 1:16-18 says, "And God made two great lights; the greater light to rule the day, and the lesser light to rule the night: he made the stars also. And God set them in the firmament of the heaven to give light upon the earth, And to rule over the day and over the night, and to divide the light from the darkness: and God saw that it was good."

This tells us that God created us to be creatures who work during the day and rest during the darkness, making it an ideal time to get alone with God because the rest of the world is at rest and quiet.

Science tells us that we have day and night because of the rotation of the earth. When half of the earth faces the sun, we have a day. Night comes when the other part of the earth faces away from the sun. This is critical for human survival because it helps ensure a uniform temperature around the globe. The planet Mercury keeps one side towards the sun with the other part in total darkness during a year. As a result, the surface temperature on the side of Mercury closest to the sun reaches 427 degrees Celsius, a temperature hot enough to melt tin. On the side facing away from the Sun, or the night side, the temperature drops to -183 degrees Celsius. This extreme would make it impossible for any kind of quality of life because a person would live in one extreme or the other.

Our life is dependent on having day and night for survival, and God uses this analogy to refer to our lives here on earth. When you are young and strong, that means things are going sunny for you, and it is a vibrant time of your life where your physical strength and stamina are at their peak. But when you are in the nighttime of your life during your twilight years, you become frail and are unable to do as much for God as you could have during your daylight hours.

Paul encouraged Timothy to be strong and not let anyone despise his youth (1 Timothy 4:12). "Let no man despise thy youth; but be thou an example of the believers, in word, in conversation, in charity, in spirit, in faith, in purity."

Some of the benefits of being a youth are: God has blessed you with time, an opportunity to increase skill and acquire knowledge, and you are generally at the peak of a healthy life, both physically and mentally. For this reason, if you want to give God the best years of your life, this is the time to do it. As a young man or woman, what would you do that you might not be able to do later in life?

There are many works we can do to promote the work of God. God has given each of us a gift or gifts to do His work.

"For to one is given the word of wisdom through the Spirit, to another the word of knowledge through the same Spirit, to another faith by the same Spirit, to another gifts of healings by the same Spirit, to another the working of miracles, to another prophecy, to another discerning of spirits, to another *different* kinds of tongues, to another the interpretation of tongues." (1 Corinthians 12:8-10)

All these gifts are for the profiting of the church. Well, will you sit down and do nothing after God has given you such gifts? It is time we demonstrate the gifts that God has given to us. There are sick people out there who need us to pray for them; we need to offer up a word of prophecy for someone to be exhorted, edified, and encouraged.

Many people have not heard about the gospel. Scripture says Satan has blinded their eyes from seeing the truth.

"But if our gospel be hid, it is hid to them that are lost: In whom the god of this world hath blinded the minds of them which believe not, lest the light of the glorious gospel of Christ, who is the image of God, should shine unto them. For we preach not ourselves, but Christ Jesus the Lord; and ourselves your servants for Jesus' sake." (2 Corinthians 4:3-5)

What can we do to help? Jesus said we should do the work of the Lord while we have the time and the strength because these things will not be available to us forever. If God is calling you to evangelize to people on a different continent, this is the time to do so while you have the strength. We have to be wise stewards with the strength and mental acuity God has given us before the night hits us.

The night is coming! There is no way that we can stop it from coming. Old age and death are part of being human beings. This is why David told us to "number our days."

David said he would seek God early, and Jesus woke up before daybreak to seek his Father. As we get older, we do not have the physical and mental stamina we had while we were younger, so let us be about, "redeeming the time because the days are evil" (Ephesians 5:16).

Chapter 3
Day and Night

When it comes to the subject of night and day, the scientific and spiritual analogies are numerous. Scientifically, the day represents the period when part of a planet faces the sun while the rest of the planet lies in the night. The sun is there, constantly shining on the planet 24/7, but what makes the difference between night and day is the rotation of the planet on its axis. For example, a single day on Mercury is 58.6 Earth days. Venus rotates so slowly that one day on this planet lasts nearly 243 Earth days. Mars is only 40 minutes longer than a day on Earth. By contrast, the gas giants, Jupiter, Saturn, Uranus, and Neptune, have days that are a fraction of an Earth day at around 9 hours, 10 hours, 17 hours, and 15 hours respectively. During each of these times, if you were to live on one of these planets, one-half of the time would be in darkness. How would you like to have to live in the dark for six months?

In Genesis 1:3-5 it records, "And God said, Let there be light: and there was light. And God saw the light, that it was good: and God divided the light from the darkness. And God called the light Day, and the darkness he called Night. And the evening and the morning were the first day."

This is not a reference to a "day" on earth with a natural period of the night because the sun and moon were not created until the fourth day.

"And God said, Let there be lights in the firmament of the heaven to divide the day from the night; and let them be for signs, and for seasons, and for days, and years: And let them be for lights in the firmament of the heaven to give light upon the earth: and it was so. And God made two great lights; the greater light to rule the day, and the lesser light to rule the night: he made the stars also." (Genesis 1:14-16)

This difference is important because, with the two passages, God established that there is a separate period he refers to as day and night that is separate from our standard period used to tell time. I will not go into the spiritual implications of how according to Psalm 19, the sun represents God while the moon represents his bride. Rather I want to focus on the principle of our lives being divided into day and night. We instinctively acknowledge this in our common vernacular. When we describe an extreme difference between two things, we say, "they are as different as night and day."

In a similar manner, there is a vast difference between the day and night portions of our lives. Like the planets, the length of these periods is different for everyone, but one thing we all have in common is night and day.

In our lives, DAY represents youth, greater light, strength, brightness, clarity, vision, health, hopes, potential, warmth, being energetic and full of life. We refer to this time as the "flower of life," or the time when flowers bloom, which is in the daytime.

NIGHT, on the other hand, represents weakness, lesser light, old age, sickness, frailty, coldness, and death. While it is possible to see a blinding light and we can feel the sun's warmth, anyone who has been alone on a moonless night someplace where there are no stars or light pollution from civilization can tell you the darkness is so terrifying that you almost "feel it." By contrast, when you "feel" the day, it brings forth thoughts of comfort and peace.

Oswald Mbuyiseni Mtshali, a South African poet, described this concept of nightfall in his poem, *Nightfall in Soweto*. I love his simple yet profound description of the night.

Nightfall comes like
a dreaded disease
seeping through the pores
of a healthy body
and ravaging it beyond repair

Nightfall symbolizes insecurity and fear. Up in Alaska near the North Pole, the nights and days are six months long because of the earth's tilt. When the darkness comes, you lock yourself in your cabin and don't go out until the light returns. During this time, the Polar Bears come out of their hibernation and roam about the darkness freely. If you ask any zoologist, they will tell you these are the most terrifying of all species of bear. The night is terrifying for these people, with some even being known to commit suicide over having to be away from the light for so long. I believe people living in this spiritual fear that the darkness brings wish they could bask in the daytime forever.

This principle is enshrined in our future home in eternity, following the millennial reign of Jesus Christ. In Revelation 22:3-5, it declares, "And there shall be no more curse: but the throne of God and of the Lamb shall be in it; and his servants shall serve him: And they shall see his face; and his name shall be in their foreheads. **And there shall be no night there; and they need no candle, neither light of the sun; for the Lord God giveth them light**: and they shall reign for ever and ever."

The two great lights teach us a lesson. God made the greater light to rule the day because daytime is when most human activity occurs. Historically, almost nothing of significance occurred during the evening hours because of a lack of artificial light. Even today, the vast majority of businesses keep daylight hours. We use the phrase "banker's hours" to refer to this time.

Daylight hours are the best time to go after something you desire. The atmosphere is clear, your vision is able to see much farther on earth, and you derive energy from the daylight.

God refers to the evening as a period when the "Lesser light to rule the night." This lesser light is the moon, which reflects light instead of generating its own light (Job 25:5). You are limited in your ability to accomplish things where there is much less light. During darkness, before modern technology such as night googles came along, travel was hindered at night and much slower because you were limited by how far you could see. God, in His infinite wisdom, created a night to have a lesser amount of power and ability to aid us because our accomplishments are limited and diminished when it is nighttime.

Even though we now live in an age where artificial light has enabled us to work around the clock, scientific studies continue to reveal that human beings are more productive when it is daytime and less productive at night.

If that is the case when it comes to accomplishing physical work, which period do you think would be the best time to seek God? The answer, of course, would be during the daylight hours.

This is the best time to seek God and to do His work. This is the best time to go after your dreams and visions when you are fresh and rejuvenated. What are your dreams? What are your visions? Do you have any? If you do, then this is the time to start pursuing them. Everyone has dreams and visions, so do not waste time. There is a difference between having a dream and a vision. A dream is some lofty pie-in-the-sky thing that you would enjoy having, but you never take any steps to bring to fruition. By contrast, a vision may contain all the elements of a dream, but it inspires you to create a plan and goals to bring it to pass.

When you are working at fulfilling the vision God has given you, be sure not to compare yourself to others. Paul stated in 2 Corinthians 10:12, "For we dare not make ourselves of the number, or compare ourselves with some that commend themselves: but they measuring themselves by themselves, and comparing themselves among themselves, are not wise."

I realize it is part of our human nature to use our five senses and compare ourselves to others, but we need to remember that we are to fight and work in the spiritual realm, or, like Abraham, we are to walk by faith, not by sight. Paul says when we compare ourselves to others, we are foolish.

Use whatever strength God has given you now while it is the day for you, for there will come a time in your life when you will no longer be able to work with the fervency and intensity you were able to do during your younger years.

That period of time will be different for everybody. Some people are able to go with full vigor and energy into their 50s and 60s, while others begin to diminish in their early 40s. Regardless of the exact year, that time will come for all of us, and it is just a matter of when. The only person I know of whom that was not said was Moses. Scripture stated, "And Moses was an hundred and twenty years old when he died: his eye was not dim, nor his natural force abated" (Deuteronomy 34:7). But it also stated that he was one-of-a-kind.

"And there arose not a prophet since in Israel like unto Moses, whom the LORD knew face to face," (Deuteronomy 34:10)

We cannot change the night when it comes. We cannot change frailty, old age, death, and loss. When the clock is against you, you might have the wisdom to start over and even have the desire to do greater things, but it will be too late because you may be frail or incapable.

When we are given the opportunity to do things for God, we should not hesitate to take advantage of it. The day is the time to repent and rededicate ourselves to God and to serve Him with all our might because we cannot do anything when we are weak or dead. Let us seek God while it is still our day.

There was a story of a young man who was very rich and handsome and married at a very young age. He traveled to many faraway lands because of his money, ate different foods, wore expensive clothing, and used expensive perfumes. He had many girlfriends besides his wife.

Because of this man's large amount of personal possessions, he assumed that because it was still a day for him, he was going to enjoy life, never bothering to waste time with thoughts of old age or death, for he had plenty of time to worry about such things.

He refused to serve God, despite many Christians sharing the word of God with him and warning him how life was like a vapor that wafted away on the wind. Each time, he would respond by dismissing their concerns, flippantly stating that he will always have more time to think about such things.

One day as he was driving one of his numerous cars, he got into a horrible accident. Another car pulled out in front of him while he was driving at a high rate of speed. In order to avoid a collision, he instinctively snapped the steering wheel to the left, causing the car to flip multiple times. When the police and paramedics arrived on the scene, the roof of his car had been completely crushed level with the dashboard, the doors were caved in, and he was wedged inside the car so tightly it took a couple of hours to safely remove him from the vehicle.

After being unconscious for days, when he finally woke up in the hospital, this young man was told that his car was totaled and he had nearly died. The doctor stated it was only by a miracle that he was still alive today. However, his injuries were very severe. He was in a full-body cast, and his legs were amputated. When he wanted to scream, he discovered he was not able to speak. He could see and hear, and move his arms and hands, so he asked for a pen and paper.

He wrote: "Now I want to get closer to God. Please find me a pastor or a Christian to lead me to Jesus Christ and show me what I need to do."

Within seconds of writing the last word, he passed away into eternity. Although he had been given numerous chances to accept Jesus Christ as his personal Saviour, he never got around to it because he always thought he had plenty of time.

Up in heaven, God issues forth the final verdict on the choice this young man made with the following words as found in Scripture. "But God said unto him, Thou fool, this night thy soul shall be required of thee: then whose shall those things be, which thou hast provided?" (Luke 12:20). And "For what shall it profit a man, if he shall gain the whole world, and lose his own soul?" (Matthew 8:36).

Our time on earth is short. We shouldn't play with it. While we have the opportunity to serve Him, let us make good use of our time. Scripture warns us to "Redeeming the time, because the days are evil" (Ephesians 5:16). Time is the most precious asset and commodity you own, for you cannot replace or earn any more of it. Once it is expended, it is gone forever, never to be seen again.

If you are planning on doing something, do it while it is the day for you. Get married while you are still young so you can enjoy the wife or spouse of your youth (Proverbs 5:18). Go to school, start that business, learn that skill. Do not wait for your night to come.

Pursue your dreams while you have the strength and a sound mind. Young man and young woman, do not waste your day. Start it now. Procrastination is the thief of time. Postponing dreams and visions can destroy one's life. We do not have much time on earth. "Man who is born of a woman is few of days and full of trouble" (Job 14:1).

Think about this verse. If your days on earth are short, what kind of a person will you be? You should not be about wasting your time. "Why stand ye here all the day idle?" (Matthew 20:6). Do something to better your life. There is a message in you that God wants to use you to bring to the world. God is waiting to use you to proclaim His gospel.

There is a message that people have to hear. The gospel must be preached to people all over the world. God is calling you. Now that you have the strength, it is time to answer the call of God. Do not wait for your old age before you do something for God.

Chapter 4
Limited at Night

We all have limitations. God is the only one without limitations. Even the angels have limitations. Man is hindered at night as compared to day for performing the daily activities of life. This is the way God made us. At night, at the end of a hard day's work, we put away our work tools and dreams until the next day. We draw the day to a close and then go home, where we kick back and relax for a short time before going to sleep and starting the cycle all over again the next day. When the day comes to a close, many workplaces shut their doors, especially smaller businesses and those that provide services such as an attorney or auto mechanic.

Many people find it difficult to drive at night, and as you get older, you may develop what is known as nyctalopia (night blindness), where you find it difficult to see when the headlights of an approaching car cause your pupils to dilate.

When it rains, it can be almost impossible to see the stripes separating the lanes.

It is because men find it difficult to perform effectively at night. When given a choice, all other things being equal regarding wages, etc., most people prefer to work during the day and have their evenings free to sleep during the night. People who work the midnight shift often have issues getting quality sleep during the day. They need to trick their bodies by having their bedrooms be in complete darkness; if not, their body fights to get Rapid Eye Movement deep sleep.

Most of life's daily activities normally occur during the day, such as going to school, taking your children to a park, family outings, and many more things that happen during the daytime.

On the other hand, when it comes to winter, while many exciting things can be done, such as skiing and ice skating, it can also be a challenging time, as anyone who has had to drive through a blizzard or ice storm can attest to.

The wisest man who ever lived provided us with a powerful illustration regarding the ant and how they prepare for the upcoming winter each year.

"Go to the ant, thou sluggard; consider her ways, and be wise: Which having no guide, overseer, or ruler, provided her meat in the summer, and gathereth her food in the harvest. How long wilt thou sleep, O sluggard? When wilt thou arise out of thy sleep? Yet a little sleep, a little slumber, a little folding of the hands to sleep: So shall thy poverty come as one that travelleth, and thy want as an armed man." (Proverbs 6:6-11)

Kidsgen.com has a great children's song illustrating this truth that is very powerful and very informative. On their website, they narrated a story about how one summer day, a Grasshopper was hopping about, chirping and singing merrily. Then he saw an ant passing by, carrying an ear of corn to his anthill. The grasshopper inquired of the little ant, "Why not come and chat with me?"

The ant refused and explained, "I am helping my fellow ants by laying up food for the winter, and you should do the same."

The grasshopper said with a dismissive tone, "Why should I bother about the winters? We have got plenty of food at present. In fact, we have more than we need, so what's the worry?"

But the ant went on its way and continued to gather food. A few months later, when the harsh winter came, it wasn't long before the grasshopper had no food and found himself dying of hunger. Yet, he could look over at the anthill and hear sounds of joy when each day he watched the ants distributing to each other all the corn and grain in their stores they had collected in the summer.

Desperate and ready to perish, the grasshopper went to the ant and asked for food. The ant refused and said, "You should have worked during the summer months in summers rather than just sitting and singing while others did all the work."

The moral behind this story is to be wise and safe, and during the summer, you need to gather and plan ahead for winter. Save food, build a home for yourself and your family. Winter in this story represents your old age, along with the times of uncertainty and difficult times this period of your life will bring. You may have a longer summer period than someone else, but regardless of how long this portion of your life is, it will not last forever.

There will come a day when the wind will slowly start to blow and when you wake up, the temperature will not be as warm as it was the day before. You will start to notice a slight frost on your windows, and the days will start getting shorter. As things continue, one morning, you will discover ice on the puddle in front of your house, and the sun is farther away. There will be many days when you can see the circle of the sun clearly because the clouds filter out the intense ultraviolet light that warmed you during the summer. Then the air itself will have a cold snap that only intensifies when the wind blows. This will be followed by the snow that coats the ground, making driving treacherous.

No matter how long summer will last, winter will surely come. What can we learn from all of this?

Years ago, a preacher who had an amazing talent to do chalk drawings while preaching had an amazing message he preached all over the country titled, *The Measure of a Man.*

He began by drawing the picture of the face of a cute little newborn baby. He went on to explain how there is nothing more amazing than a baby. They are so innocent, and they have their whole life in front of them.

Then he changed the face to that of a young five-year-old. He explained that now this young boy had first heard about God and the Bible stories, but he wasn't sure what to do about it.

Then the boy became a teenager who did all the things teens do. This young person was familiar with the gospel and the importance of serving God, but he thought to himself, I'll do that later; right now, I just want to have some fun.

Then he changed the picture into that of a young man, followed by a middle-aged man. He explained that the Holy Spirit spoke to him along each stage of this person's life, encouraging him to come to Christ for salvation and then go on to serve him. But each time, he rebuffed the Spirit's entreaties, and each time the voice became quieter and more distant.

Finally, the picture morphed into an old man at the end of his life. He said, "By now, the Holy Spirits is so distant the man can barely hear him. In fear, he asks, 'are you still there, Lord.' To which the Lord responds, but his heart has been so hardened now that he just ignores it, like he had always done."

He would then close with an invitation, asking the audience which stage of this person's life they were at. Then he reminded them that the Lord is calling out to them, just like he did with the person in this story through each stage of life. He said the fact they were here and listening to this sermon meant the Lord was still calling them, and then he asked them to make a decision.

One particular time, after preaching the message and after everyone had left the auditorium, he was cleaning up all his chalk and getting things together when he noticed an old man standing there quietly in front of the image. Sensing the man was under some kind of deep conviction, he walked over and said, "What's up, pops?"

Without looking down, still staring directly at the picture, the man said, "Preacher, you done drawing my picture."

Stunned, he said, "Well, sir, the man in that picture is lost and on his way to Hell. If you're saying that's you, then you need to be saved. I told you what you have to do to be saved in the message. I'll help share the scriptures with you if you want. Wouldn't you like to be saved?"

The old man just shook his head, to which the preacher replied, "Why don't you want to get saved? It's evident by your age that you're in your twilight years. You've got most of your years behind you. What's stopping you from trusting Christ?"

The old man, still staring at the picture, just said in a monotone, "Well, I guess it's like I said, you done drawing my picture." Then he walked away without saying another word.

While you are still young is time to work and secure yourself well for your future. Do not play around while you are strong. Remember, winter, which is your old age, is coming. As Paul was nearing the date of his execution at the hand of the evil Roman Emperor, Nero implored Timothy to "Do thy diligence to come before winter" (2 Timothy 4:21). Scripture never records if Timothy made it in time or not. I wonder if he made it. Come before winter.

Chapter 5
What Will You Do During Your Daytime?

Accepting Jesus Christ as your personal Saviour is the most important thing you can ever do. While there are many important events in her life, such as who we pick for our friends, what college, if any, we decide to go to, who we marry, our choice of career and city where we live, and the financial decisions we make. All these things are important and life-changing. However, they pale in comparison to how you answer the question Jesus asked in Matthew 22:42. "What think ye of Christ? whose son is he?" Your answer to this question is so important that it will determine where you will spend eternity, in heaven or hell.

This decision must be made while you are in the daytime of your life. In this case, daytime meaning while you are still alive and in this body of flesh. Once you are dead, there are no second chances at the final judgment. God's verdict will be based on one simple thing, what did you do with his son?

Jesus explained how important this was when he had a conversation with a religious leader of his day named Nicodemus. This man was well-versed in the available scriptures of his day. If anybody had known how to get to heaven after he died, it would have been Nicodemus. But let's eavesdrop on this conversation.

There was a man of the Pharisees, named Nicodemus, a ruler of the Jews: The same came to Jesus by night, and said unto him, Rabbi, we know that thou art a teacher come from God: for no man can do these miracles that thou doest, except God be with him.

Jesus answered and said unto him, Verily, verily, I say unto thee, Except a man be born again, he cannot see the kingdom of God.

Nicodemus saith unto him, How can a man be born when he is old? Can he enter the second time into his mother's womb and be born?

Jesus answered, "Verily, verily, I say unto thee, Except a man be born of water and of the Spirit, he cannot enter into the kingdom of God. That which is born of the flesh is flesh; and that which is born of the Spirit is spirit. Marvel not that I said unto thee, Ye must be born again. The wind bloweth where it listeth, and thou hearest the sound thereof, but canst not tell whence it cometh, and whither it goeth: so is every one that is born of the Spirit."

Nicodemus answered and said unto him, "How can these things be?"

Jesus answered and said unto him, "Art thou a master of Israel, and knowest not these things? Verily, verily, I say unto thee, We speak that we do know, and testify that we have seen; and ye receive not our witness. If I have told you earthly things, and ye believe not, how shall ye believe, if I tell you of heavenly things? And no man hath ascended up to heaven, but he that came down from heaven, even the Son of man which is in heaven. And as Moses lifted up the serpent in the wilderness, even so must the Son of man be lifted up: That whosoever believeth in him should not perish, but have eternal life." (John 3:1-15)

Notice that Jesus said the problem has to do with our genes, and therefore, he said we need to be "born again."

God is a Trinity, therefore Adam was made a three-part being with a body, soul, and spirit (1 Thessalonians 5:23). God placed Adam eastward in a garden in Eden and gave him a single job, to tend and keep it.

The man was given just one prohibition; he was not to partake of the fruit from the tree of good and evil knowledge. God warned, "in the day thou eatest thereof, thou shalt surely die." This prohibition and warning were very clear. However, as we read in Genesis 3, Adam and his wife Eve broke this prohibition, causing sin to enter the world and mar all of creation (Romans 8:22). Yet, despite God's clear warning that Adam would die the very day he ate the fruit, Adam lived another 900+ years before he died. This seems to be a contradiction, but we know that God cannot lie, and His word will never fail. So exactly what happened?

To answer this question, we must remember what we have discussed so far, that Adam was created a three-part being representing the Trinity. The three parts include a body, soul, and spirit. The body is nothing more than an outward shell, similar to how a house is created to provide a dwelling place for individuals to live in.

The Bible describes the soul as a living creature that dwells inside the body, much like the homeowner. In Genesis 35:18, when Rachel died after giving birth to Benjamin, it said, "And it came to pass, as her soul was in departing, (for she died)..." We know her earthly body was buried on earth so what departed was something else. When John saw the fifth seal opened in Revelation 6:9, he said, "I saw under the altar the souls of them that were slain for the word of God, and for the testimony which they held."

In Luke 16, Jesus tells us a story about a pair of men who died, a poor man named Lazarus, and an unnamed rich man. Contrary to what some have claimed, this is not a parable. We know this because, in each of the parables, scripture plainly declares that they are parables. Also, in each of the parables, Jesus afterward explains what each object or individual in the parable represents. Finally, he never mentions an individual by name, instead of saying things like, "a certain man," but in Luke 16, he mentions Lazarus by name; something is done in none of the parables. Let's see what happens to these two individuals after death, and their soul leaves their body.

"And it came to pass, that the beggar died, and was carried by the angels into Abraham's bosom: the rich man also died, and was buried; And in hell he lift up his eyes, being in torments, and seeth Abraham afar off, and Lazarus in his bosom. And he cried and said, Father Abraham, have mercy on me, and send Lazarus, that he may dip the tip of his finger in water, and cool my tongue; for I am tormented in this flame." (Luke 16:22-24)

In these passages, we see that the rich man had eyes and a tongue, while Lazarus had fingers. Again, notice that a soul has a bodily shape, and it is something that departs the body following death to either be with God or goes to hell.

As we can see, even after Adam's fall, human beings have a body and a soul, so these parts of our original three-part image did not die, so that leaves Adam's spirit as the part that died that day. Adam's disobedience marred and destroyed that part of the image of God in him. This is why the Apostle Paul said in the great resurrection chapter of first Corinthians

15, "and so what is written, the first man Adam was made a living soul; the last Adam [Jesus] was made a quickening (or living) spirit." Notice he did not say that Jesus was made a living body or soul following the resurrection, although his body was brought back to life, never to die again. Every word in scripture is placed there for a specific purpose.

Because of this missing part of Adam's three-part original creation, every person born since then is no longer born in the image of God as Adam was when he was created, meaning a three-part being. Rather we are born in the image of Adam. We see this in Genesis 5:3, where the word of God says that Adam "begat a son in his own likeness." As a result of having this missing part that is supposed to be there, human beings go through life with a natural yearning and desire to restore that missing part of their image, which enabled them to have that sweet fellowship in the garden Adam shared with the Lord.

It is for this reason that Jesus, our second Adam, gave his life to restore the image of God in the earth through his obedience. His death brought new life through salvation and restored our relationship with God by enabling our dead spirit to resurrect and once again become alive. Those who are born again have that threefold part that Adam once had, while those who are lost and unsaved are only a two-part being.

The only way this can happen is for us to be born with having the image of Jesus Christ.

One of the greatest verses in the Bible is John 3:16, which states, "For God so loved the world, that he gave his only begotten Son, that whosoever believeth in him should not perish, but have everlasting life."

However, this verse's good news has caused some to think that since God is so loving, there is no hurry to worry about this verse, like the man in our illustration earlier who was in the car accident. God loves me, so he knows I want to do it one day, so he will give me plenty of time, people reason.

However, going back to what we showed, the scripture teaches about our being born in Adam's image, not God's; there is another important verse in John 3 that indicates the urgency of trusting Christ NOW!

"He that believeth on the Son hath everlasting life: and he that believeth not the Son shall not see life; but the wrath of God abideth on him." (John 3:36)

Notice this verse is in the present tense, which is why it was so important for Jesus Christ, who the Bible says was "God manifest in the flesh," to come to earth and die for the sins of his creation.

As God, and the one whom we wronged by our sin, He has sole discretion to set the terms and conditions for how we are permitted to come back to him. This is why Jesus declared in John 14:6, "Jesus saith unto him, "I am the WAY the TRUTH and the LIFE, no man cometh to the father but by me."

So how exactly do we come to Jesus? Fortunately, God did not leave us having to guess the answer to this question. Nor did he make it vague so that religious leaders can offer up their own ideas without us having any way to verify if they are telling the truth or not or who is right and who is wrong. You have probably heard some people say things such as you need to be baptized to be saved; you need to keep the commandments until the end of your life to get to heaven. You must join a particular church, along with trusting Jesus or some other claims.

However, if we want to find out the right way, we should heed Jesus' admonition to "search the scriptures."

The scriptures declare that the Apostle Paul was the "apostle to the gentiles" (Romans 11:13). In the Bible, during Paul's day, people were considered divided into two groups, Jews and Gentiles. So this means Paul is our Apostle.

While the entire Bible has been given to us to learn from, we should pay attention to what Paul has to say about salvation. In fact, Paul felt this issue was so important he wrote an entire book on the subject. In the Book of Romans (gentiles), Paul gives several verses that provide a spiritual roadmap for salvation.

"As it is written, There is none righteous, no, not one: (Romans 3:10)

"For all have sinned, and come short of the glory of God;" (Romans 3:23)

These verses can best be summed up by the old adage, "nobody's perfect." Simply stated, it says that whoever we are, no matter how good we may be, all of us come short of God's holy standard of perfection. Just like in basketball, where some may narrowly miss making a basket when the ball dances on the rim before falling away, or whether someone misses the backboard completely, a miss is still a miss.

Because we miss God's mark, what is the payment for sin?

"For the wages of sin is death; but the gift of God is eternal life through Jesus Christ our Lord." (Romans 6:23)

A wage is a payment for services rendered. When we get a paycheck, it is something we have earned. The Bible declares that the payment for our sin is death. However, this does not just mean physical death because we will all die one day.

The Bible shows us that there is more than one death.

"And death and hell were cast into the lake of fire. This is the second death. And whosoever was not found written in the book of life was cast into the lake of fire." (Revelation 20:14-15)

The question then becomes, if the wages of sin is death in the lake of fire, exactly which sins will land a person in this place?

"But the fearful, and unbelieving, and the abominable, and murderers, and whoremongers, and sorcerers, and idolaters, and all liars, shall have their part in the lake which burneth with fire and brimstone: which is the second death." (Revelation 21:8)

While the list of sins includes many of what we would consider "really bad" sins, notice God placed the word "all" before only a single sin in the list. That sin is "all liars."

How many lies does a person have to tell to be a liar? The same number as how many murders a person has to commit to be considered a murderer, one. So we can see that based on God's criteria, just a single sin has a sentence of eternity in the lake of fire.

If you think all seems hopeless at this point, let not your heart be troubled, for Paul had this to say.

"But God commendeth his love toward us, in that, while we were yet sinners, Christ died for us." (Romans 5:8)

The word "commendeth" means proved or demonstrated. In other words, like they say, "talk is cheap." But God didn't just say he loved you; he proved it by sending his Son, Jesus Christ, to die for us. This is why the last half of Romans 6:23 says, "but the gift of God is eternal life through Jesus Christ our Lord."

Paul also said the same thing in Ephesians 2:8-9. "For by grace are ye saved through faith; and that not of yourselves: it is the gift of God: Not of works, lest any man should boast."

Unlike a wage, a gift is not something you work for or earn. It is something that is totally undeserved that someone gives to you of their own free will. God is offering you a free gift today, right now. That gift is eternal life, and it only comes through the finished work of Jesus Christ on Calvary.

So how do you appropriate or receive this gift?

"For there is no difference between the Jew and the Greek: for the same Lord over all is rich unto all that call upon him. For whosoever shall call upon the name of the Lord shall be saved." (Romans 10:12-13)

The answer is simple, you simply call on the name of the Lord, in sincerity, not just to repeat a prayer, and receive the free gift Jesus is offering you today.

While a prayer will never save anybody, if you are having trouble grasping what to say to God since this is all new to you, you could say something like this; but again, what matters is your heart motive.

"Heavenly Father, I come to you in the name of Jesus. Your word says that everyone who calls on the name of the Lord will be saved. Today, the best way I know how, I am calling on you. I pray and ask Jesus to come into my heart and be the Lord of my life according to Romans 10:9-10, which says, "That if thou shalt confess with thy mouth the Lord Jesus, and shalt believe in thine heart that God hath raised him from the dead, thou shalt be saved. For with the heart man believeth unto righteousness; and with the mouth confession is made unto salvation."

Once you have prayed that prayer, understanding what you just did and meaning it, based on the authority of the word of God, written by the King of the universe who does not lie, you are now reborn in the image of Jesus Christ, just as I was. Like me, you are now a Christian, a child of the Almighty God!

It is not the end-all, however. While works do not save you, God has a purpose for your life beyond just saving your soul from hell. Following Ephesians 2:8-9 comes verse 10, which states, "For we are his workmanship, created in Christ Jesus unto good works, which God hath before ordained that we should walk in them."

In other words, God wants you to give your life to him and serve him. Paul talked about this in Romans 12:1-2.

"I beseech you therefore, brethren, by the mercies of God, that ye present your bodies a living sacrifice, holy, acceptable unto God, which is your reasonable service. And be not conformed to this world: but be ye transformed by the renewing of your mind, that ye may prove what is that good, and acceptable, and perfect, will of God." (Romans 12:1-2)

Notice that Paul said this is your "reasonable service." After all that Jesus did for you, even though works do not save you, it is not unreasonable for him to ask you to live for him.

It is not something to be put off. It must be done while you are in your daytime. Paul said, "For he saith, I have heard thee in a time accepted, and in the day of salvation have I succoured thee: behold, now is the accepted time; behold, now is the day of salvation" (2 Corinthians 6:2).

I always tell people that while you have the strength to talk, it is the best time to confess sins and call upon Jesus. When you do, you will be saved.

Our salvation is very important, but we need to work on it by doing our part in our calling for Jesus. In Philippians 2:12, Paul states, "Wherefore, my beloved, as ye have always obeyed, not as in my presence only, but now much more in my absence, work out your own salvation with fear and trembling. For it is God which worketh in you both to will and to do of his good pleasure."

While you are in your day, that is the best time to make the great decision of inviting Jesus Christ into your life.

"He cometh forth like a flower, and is cut down: he fleeth also as a shadow, and continueth not." (Job 14:2)

"For all flesh is as grass, and all the glory of man as the flower of grass. The grass withereth, and the flower thereof falleth away: But the word of the Lord endureth for ever. And this is the word which by the gospel is preached unto you." (1 Peter 1:24-25)

Think or meditate on these bible scriptures. A beautiful lady is not going to be young and beautiful forever on this earth. You might be able to apply makeup and have plastic surgery to maintain your youthful appearance like many celebrities do, but remember this, "ladies, you can't fool a flight of stairs." And for all those young men who got a chuckle out of this, don't worry, I haven't forgotten about you. All those muscles you have put on by working out will turn to the fat one day as you get older, and your hairline will recede.

Everything is passing quickly. Therefore make good use of your time and your day while you still have it. When you are in your day and are blossoming like a flower, be fruitful, vigilant, and stick to God's word. Do not let salvation depart from your house.

This is the gospel and the great news for everyone. Jesus Christ, the son of God who became man, had no sin and was crucified and died on the cross, buried and was raised from the dead by God (1 Corinthians 15:1-8).

Jesus died to bring us to God. He is calling you today to join God's family.

"But as many as received him, to them gave he power to become the sons of God, even to them that believe on his name:" (John 1:12)

"For God so loved the world, that he gave his only begotten Son, that whosoever believeth in him should not perish, but have everlasting life. For God sent not his Son into the world to condemn the world; but that the world through him might be saved. He that believeth on him is not condemned: but he that believeth not is condemned already, because he hath not believed in the name of the only begotten Son of God." (John 3:16-18)

There is eternal life for us all, but first, you have to accept Jesus Christ as your personal Saviour and believe in Him.

Today is your time of salvation. Do not harden your heart. For tomorrow is not guaranteed. Now is the time to make this decision to follow Jesus. Let Him come to your heart, and He will change your life, and you will have eternal life.

Chapter 6
Twelve Hours

In John 11:9-10, we read, "Jesus answered, Are there not twelve hours in the day? If any man walk in the day, he stumbleth not, because he seeth the light of this world. But if a man walk in the night, he stumbleth, because there is no light in him."

This statement from Jesus Christ is very powerful. He made it in response to his disciples' concern about returning to Jerusalem after receiving a request to go and help one of their dear friends, a man named Lazarus. It was no secret that the religious leaders were looking to entrap Jesus and seeking a way to put him to death. This caused the disciples to be concerned, wondering if perhaps it would be better if they all went there at a more convenient time.

When Jesus answered them, he was using the illustration of a traveler going to a different city. It is hard for us to comprehend today when we can climb into a car and in 12 hours drive nearly halfway across the country. In Jesus' time, while an individual could certainly cover a respectable distance on horseback or on a mule, this was not the primary travel method. For one thing, these animals require a lot of maintenance in the sense that you would need to carry food and water for them. Moreover, a poor person would not have access to such a luxury.

A reading of the Gospels shows that the primary method of travel for the disciples, along with many of the people during Jesus' day, was by foot. When your sole method of travel is walking, you are greatly limited in how far you can go in a day during the daylight hours

If you are on a lengthy journey, you will plan ahead regarding the places where you would stop for the night. Unlike today, where everything is well lit in the evenings if you found yourself between cities in the evening, it was completely pitch black. Not only that, the area you were in was often the home of roving bands of robbers and marauders. These individuals knew the land's layout far more than you did and could easily sneak up on you in the middle of the night and rob and kill you.

While traveling in the daytime, a man would be able to see and avoid any obstacles or dangers and not stumble because he had the light of the sun to guide him, even if he was in unfamiliar territory. However, while traveling at nighttime, he would be unable to see many of the dangers around him due to his limited vision.

If God has given us twelve hours in a day to see clearly compared to having to walk in darkness, then why not take advantage of this blessing and decide to walk or travel in the day, only walking in the evening when necessity demands it. Why not begin implementing the dreams and/or visions God has given us during the daytime when it is much easier to do. A good example is planning for retirement. If an individual takes steps early in life, during the daylight when they are in their late teens, and remains faithful in preparation for that day that is decades off in the future during their nighttime; it is much easier, and the chances are in their favor that they will have much more available to them for retirement then if they wait to start doing it when they are in their 50s.

The same is true when it comes to building up your heavenly retirement account. The time to begin earning rewards in heaven is during your daylight hours when you have the opportunity to bank many of them up where they will compound interest.

In case you're wondering what I mean by this because it is probably something you've never heard before, I would like to call your attention to 2 John 1:8. "Look to yourselves, that we lose not those things which we have wrought, but that we receive a full reward."

Notice that John addresses the people in this church and tells them as individuals to look to themselves regarding their walk with the Lord and service for him. Normally we would expect a person to say they should do these things to make sure they don't lose rewards at The Judgment Seat of Christ. However, John is asking them to continue serving God so that he doesn't lose rewards during that time.

To understand how this can be, we need to look at the verse that discusses rewards for the Christian, as opposed to the lost at the Great White throne judgment.

"For other foundation can no man lay than that is laid, which is Jesus Christ. Now if any man build upon this foundation gold, silver, precious stones, wood, hay, stubble; Every man's work shall be made manifest: for the day shall declare it, because it shall be revealed by fire; and the fire shall try every man's work of what sort it is. If any man's work abide which he hath built thereupon, he shall receive a reward. If any man's work shall be burned, he shall suffer loss: but he himself shall be saved; yet so as by fire." (1 Corinthians 3:11-15)

Notice that this judgment has nothing to do with salvation because it plainly states, "If any man's work shall be burned, he shall suffer loss: but he himself shall be saved; yet so as by fire."

However, the works we do after salvation will be put into a fire, and those things that are done for Jesus, as opposed to self, will remain, but everything else will be burned. Those things that remain are what John is referring to.

While we will certainly receive rewards for those things that we do, it also carries on in the works of those we influence. Let me give you a good example. The Apostle Paul gave his life to share the gospel with the world until it eventually resulted in his martyrdom. While Paul was living, he was certainly gathering rewards for those he led to Christ. However, God cannot give Paul a full tally yet because people are still being saved as a result of Paul's missionary work.

The same is true of any Christian since then who shares the gospel. Because of modern technology, preachers who died decades ago are still being heard preaching the gospel on the radio and on the Internet. People are still hearing these messages and being saved, or after salvation having their lives transformed to do greater service for Jesus. Because of this, these individuals are still earning rewards up in heaven.

Because of this, just like the principle of compound interest, the best thing you can do to achieve the maximum number of rewards is to begin early, during the daylight hours of your life.

Many people in this world have needs that you can help fulfill. The time to help them is while they are alive. Be generous to the poor; share your bread and clothes with them while they are alive. A dead person does not need any help. There is an old gospel song titled, *Give Me Flowers While I'm Living*, which talks about how the time to show you appreciate a person is while they are here to see it rather than at their funeral.

Show love to people while they are alive. The sands of time are dwindling fast, and night is rapidly approaching. Jesus knew the time and seasons. This is why he implored us to be about doing things in the daytime.

Doing things in the daytime can also be part of our preparation for the night. Jesus told a story in Matthew 25:1-13 that illustrates this.

Then shall the kingdom of heaven be likened unto ten virgins, which took their lamps, and went forth to meet the bridegroom.

And five of them were wise, and five were foolish. The foolish ones took their lamps and took no oil with them: But the wise took oil in their vessels with their lamps.

While the bridegroom tarried, they all slumbered and slept. And at midnight, there was a cry made, Behold, the bridegroom cometh; go ye out to meet him.

Then all those virgins arose and trimmed their lamps. And the foolish said unto the wise, Give us of your oil; for our lamps are gone out.

But the wise answered, saying, Not so; lest there be not enough for us and you: but go ye rather to them that sell, and buy for yourselves.

And while they went to buy, the bridegroom came; and they that were ready went in with him to the marriage: and the door was shut.

Afterward came also the other virgins, saying, Lord, Lord, open to us. But he answered and said, Verily I say unto you, I know you not. Watch therefore, for ye know neither the day nor the hour wherein the Son of man cometh.

Preparation is important as it helps in self-control. When we take time to prepare ourselves diligently and early, it will help us stand strong when facing unexpected situations in our lives. We have to prepare during the daytime like the five wise virgins. The military has an excellent way of putting it. "The more you sweat in peacetime, the less you bleed in war."

There is an old spiritual song that illustrates this truth.

Work, For The Night Is Coming

by Lowell Mason

Work, for the night is coming

Work thro' the morning hours

Work while the dew is sparkling

Work amid springing flowers

Work when the day grows brighter

Work in the glowing sun

Work, for the night is coming

When man's work is done

Work, for the night is coming

Work thro' the sunny noon

Fill brightest hours with labor

Rest comes sure and soon

Give every flying minute

Something to keep in store

Work, for the night is coming

When man works no more

Work, for the night is coming

Under the sunset skies

While their bright tints are glowing

Work, for daylight flies

Work till the last beam fadeth

Fadeth to shine no more

Work, while the night is darkening

When man's work is over

Chapter 7

The Time of Your Salvation is Today

"For all our days are passed away in thy wrath: we spend our years as a tale that is told. The days of our years are threescore years and ten; and if by reason of strength they be fourscore years, yet is their strength labor and sorrow; for it is soon cut off, and we fly away. Who knoweth the power of thine anger? even according to thy fear, so is thy wrath. So teach us to number our days, that we may apply our hearts unto wisdom." (Psalm 90:9-12)

"Seeing his days are determined, the number of his months are with thee, thou hast appointed his bounds that he cannot pass;" (Job 14:5)

The Bible teaches that when we are born, God gives us a certain number of days we will be alive on this earth.

No one knows this number; however, we are told there are certain things we can do to lengthen or shorten this number. For example, consider Exodus 20:12. "Honour thy father and thy mother: that thy days may be long upon the land which the LORD thy God giveth thee."

This verse is true no matter what. The question then becomes, "Well I know a child who was always obedient to their parents, but they died when they were eight years old. How can this verse possibly be true when my friend's child died?"

This is why the proper method of Bible study is to compare scripture with scripture (Isaiah 28:10-13). The answer is this, "God gave that child a certain number of days when he was born. While we don't know what that number was, it was less than the date on which he died. For example, God may have numbered his days to die at age four, but because he obeyed Exodus 20:12, God extended those days by doubling them to eight years. So his days were long on the earth compared to what he had initially."

Each night brings us closer to our death. There is an uplifting gospel song titled, *I've Got One Less Day to Go*. The chorus goes like this.

> *I've got one more day behind me*
> *How many are left I don't know*
> *But I'm getting closer to Jesus*
> *I've got one less day to go*

Remember what the scripture says: "While it is said, To day if ye will hear his voice, harden not your hearts, as in the provocation." (Hebrews 3:15)

Confess your sins; ask Jesus Christ for the forgiveness of those sins. Invite Him into your heart.

"That if thou shalt confess with thy mouth the Lord Jesus, and shalt believe in thine heart that God hath raised him from the dead, thou shalt be saved. For with the heart man believeth unto righteousness; and with the mouth confession is made unto salvation. For the scripture saith, Whosoever believeth on him shall not be ashamed." (Romans 10:9-11)

"For God so loved the world, that he gave his only begotten Son, that whosoever believeth in him should not perish, but have everlasting life. For God sent not his Son into the world to condemn the world; but that the world through him might be saved. He that believeth on him is not condemned: but he that believeth not is condemned already, because he hath not believed in the name of the only begotten Son of God." (John 3:16-18)

Jesus is the only way to have everlasting life. Imagine living someday in a perfect place without disease, death, loss, or violence. A place where it says that there is "no night there." Wouldn't that be wonderful after all the sorrow, trials, and heartache we have to face here on earth?

But before we can experience these wonderful promises that God has given us, we need to pass through the doorway to heaven the right way. Many people will tell you they know the way, and it is different than anybody else's way, but to sort it out, the best thing you can do is go right to the source and read the scriptures for yourself.

When you do, you will discover that the right way to everlasting life is through a person, our Lord Jesus Christ. He died for our sins so that we can have access to everlasting life. Make Jesus your priority today, not tomorrow, for tomorrow is not yours. Jesus is calling you today!

"And if it seem evil unto you to serve the LORD, choose you this day whom ye will serve; whether the gods which your fathers served that were on the other side of the flood, or the gods of the Amorites, in whose land ye dwell: but as for me and my house, we will serve the LORD." (Joshua 24:15)

Whom will you serve? God or man? The choice is yours but choose wisely, for your eternal fate depends on it.

Reference

https://www.kidsgen.com/moral_stories/the-ant-and-the-the-grasshopper.htm